MW01230091

STONECROFT ESSENTIALS

Foundations for Sharing Your Faith

Stonecroft

Unless otherwise indicated, all Scripture quotations are taken from the Holy Bible,
New Living Translation, copyright 1996, 2004, 2015 by Tyndale House Foundation.
Used by permission of Tyndale House Publishers, Inc., Carol Stream, Illinois 60188.
All rights reserved. Also used is THE HOLY BIBLE, NEW INTERNATIONAL VERSION®, NIV®
Copyright © 1973, 1978, 1984, 2011 by Biblica, Inc.®
Used by permission. All rights reserved worldwide.

Edited by: Cara Day
Designed by: Lori Bennett Design
ISBN: 979-8-218-38457-9

Produced and Distributed by:

 Stonecroft®

PO Box 8900
Kansas City, MO 64114

800.525.8627 / connections@stonecroft.org
stonecroft.org

© 2024, Stonecroft, Inc. All rights reserved. No part of this publication may be
reproduced, stored in a retrieval system, or transmitted in any form or by any
means – electronic, mechanical, photocopy, recording, or any other – except for
brief quotations in printed review, without the prior permission of the publisher.

First printing March 2024 / Printed in the United States of America

Table of Contents

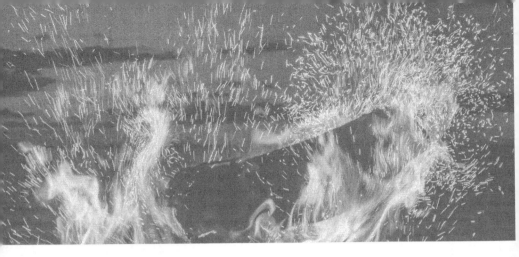

Welcome!

An ordinary spark can become an extraordinary blaze. That is God's pattern. He takes something small offered in faith and multiplies it.

Acts of prayer, of listening well, and of asking great questions have the power to connect people to God's heart, and to change lives as a result. Our seemingly mundane moments become supernatural when we invite God into them.

This guide is a tool for you to use as you go about your everyday life. It will help you remember to see people as God does, and to love them well. Whether it's the waiter or a family member, the cashier or the friend you've had forever, you'll be able to create connections and conversations that invite them to follow Jesus.

Learning to share your faith is essential at Stonecroft because we believe it's how we participate in God's sacred purpose for our lives.

Welcome to the adventure of a lifetime!

week one

Create Your Relational Map

Devote yourselves to prayer with an alert mind and a thankful heart. Pray too that God will give you many opportunities to speak about his mysterious plan concerning Christ. Pray that you will proclaim this message as clearly as you should. Live wisely among those who are not believers, and make the most of every opportunity. Let your conversation be gracious and attractive so that you will have the right response for everyone.

Colossians 4:5-6

It is not happenstance that you live where you live. God has you there for a reason and that reason is the people whose lives intersect with yours on a regular basis. Often we're not even aware of them; yet God wants to use us to make them aware of Him and the life He wants them to experience.

Ask God to open your eyes to the opportunities around you. Ask Him to help you become intentional about being His representative to the people you come in contact with each day.

On your Relational Map (*see page 9*), write your name in the middle circle; then in the circles connected to you, write in the places you frequent.

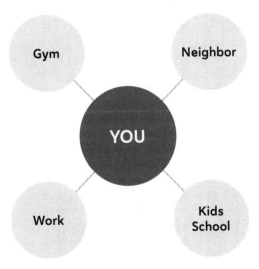

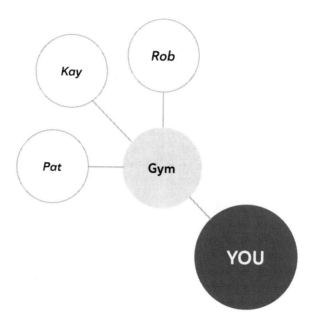

After identifying various places you go to regularly, ask God to bring to mind a few specific people in each of those places that He wants you to connect with. As He gives you these names, write them in the circles connected to the places you go. In this way, you will be forming your Relational Map.

Keep this map with your Bible or someplace where you will see it each day. Pray for the names God has given you. Maybe you don't know the names of the people God brings to mind. This will give you an excuse to introduce yourself.

Ask God to open your heart and your eyes to see how He is at work.

Pray for opportunities to make a deeper connection, to develop a friendship with them.

Ask God to give you the courage to start a faith conversation with them.

And get ready to be amazed!

My Relational Map

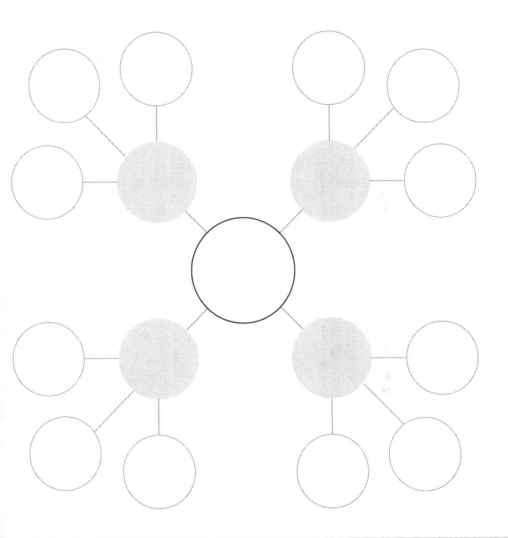

You, God, so loved the world, that You gave Your only begotten Son, that whoever believes in You shall not perish, but have eternal life. So, help me be the light in my part of the world, let my light shine before everyone I meet in such a way that they may see You.

John 3:16, Matthew 5:14-16

Evangelistic Prayer

Evangelistic prayer connects your heart to God's heart. As you seek His guidance, He will show you who He is placing in your life to love toward Jesus. And as you pray, He will provide you opportunities and ideas to build a relationship that will allow you to share your faith and mentor people in their journey to Christ.

Elements of Evangelistic Prayer

- Ask the Holy Spirit to fill you with a deep and intense desire for those who do not know Jesus. For God's light to shine through you, ask yourself:

  » Am I a vessel that God's light shines through?

  » Do I walk so close to God that others **know** it?

  » Do His love, His compassion, His grace **flow** through me?

  » To be that person, am I continually going deeper into God's Word?

    2 Corinthians 5:20: We are therefore Christ's ambassadors, as though God were making His appeal through us. We implore you on Christ's behalf: Be reconciled to God.

- Pray that God will open doors of opportunity to share the Gospel. Pray especially for those who are in your sphere of influence.

  Colossians 4:3a: Pray for us, too, that God will give us many opportunities to speak about the mysterious plan concerning Christ.

- Pray that God will show you ways to connect with lost people. Ask Him for specific names of people who do not know Jesus Christ. These people may already be in your life or God may lead you to new people to befriend. Go where **they** are; hang out with **them**.

  Colossians 4:5-6: Live wisely among those who are not believers, and make the most of every opportunity. Let your conversation be gracious and attractive so that you will have the right response for everyone.

Website to help you pray for your neighbors:
blesseveryhome.com

Listening Prayer

- Stay silent and listen. Write down the names He speaks to you.

- Ask the Holy Spirit to highlight one name from your list. Write down the name He gives you.

- Take time for silent reflection. Ask the Holy Spirit for ideas of how you might connect with the lost people around you. Write down what He gives you.

- Listen for God to show you open doors of opportunity.

> **God so loved... so we love –
> one soul at a time.**
>
> **Evangelism is not something we do;
> it is who we are.**

Praying Scripture for Those Who Do Not Yet Know Jesus

Father, in the name of Jesus, I plead that You will draw _____ to Jesus Christ in true faith and repentance. (John 6:44)

Because you came into the world to save sinners, I plead with You to save _____ who is a sinner and in need of Your grace and mercy. (I Timothy 1:13-16)

Father, give _____ a heart to know You. Draw his/her whole heart to You. (Jeremiah 24:7)

Father, I ask You to bind and remove Satan's work in _____'s life and to open _____'s eyes to the truth of the Gospel. (2 Corinthians 4:4)

Holy Spirit, I pray that You would humble _____ so that he/she sees his/her need of Jesus Christ. (Psalm 18:27; Proverbs 8:13, 29:23)

Holy Spirit, I pray that _____ will respond to your promptings and realize his/her need for Jesus Christ for personal salvation and eternal and abundant life. (II Corinthians 6:2)

Father, I pray that _____ will cease giving foothold to Satan. (Ephesians 4:27)

Lord Jesus, I pray that _____ will feel and know the burden of sin and will come to You for forgiveness, rest for his/her soul, and salvation. (Matthew 11:28-30)

Father, I pray that _____ will understand that his/her only hope for forgiveness and acceptance with You is through Jesus' work on the cross. (I Corinthians 1:18)

Holy Spirit, I pray that You would convince _____ that he/she is lost and separated from God. (Romans 3:23)

Holy Spirit, in the name of Jesus, I pray that You would destroy any false ideas that _____ has about Jesus Christ and salvation through Him. (Proverbs 14:12)

Father, I pray that You will open _____'s heart so that he/she will receive and believe the Gospel. (Acts 16:14)

Holy Spirit, I ask You through Your power and _____'s circumstances to prepare him/her to hear and receive the Word of God. (Matthew 13:1-9, 18-23)

Holy Spirit, I plead that _____ will understand the Gospel when it is presented to him/her so that the devil cannot snatch it away. (Matthew 13: 5, 9)

Holy Spirit, in the name of Jesus, I pray that the Word of God will take root in _____'s life and bring about true salvation. (Matthew 13:6, 20-21)

Father, I pray that you will deliver _____ from the kingdom of darkness and transfer _____ into the kingdom of Your dear Son. (Colossians 1:13)

Lord Jesus, I ask that _____ will not trust in himself/herself, but that _____ would completely trust in You as his/her Savior and Lord. (Galatians 2:16)

Holy God, I pray that You would grant genuine repentance to _____, a repentance that will cause him/her to hate sin and to turn from it. (Acts 11:8; Luke 13:1-3)

Lord God, I pray that You would grant _____ genuine faith, a faith that trusts in Jesus alone and surrenders to Him as Lord and Savior. (Ephesians 2:8-10)

Father, I ask that the pleasures of this world and the pressures of life will not choke the Word of God that has been sown into _____'s life. (Matthew 13:7, 22)

Father, I pray that You will continually send people into _____'s life who will proclaim the gospel clearly. (Romans 10:14)

Holy Spirit, I pray that You will cause _____ to hate sin and that You will break the power of those sins that are hindering him/her from coming to Christ. (Mark 9:43-47)

Lord, I pray that _____ will put off his/her former way of life, to be made new in the attitude of his/her mind; and to put on the new self, created to be like You, God, in true righteousness and holiness. (Ephesians 4:22-24)

Lord Jesus, I pray that _____ will not be content with the appearance of righteousness, but will seek You for the true and lasting transformation of his/her whole life. (Matthew 23:27-29)

God, I pray that _____ will receive the free gift of eternal life through Jesus Christ the Lord. (Romans 6:23)

I ask, Lord, that You will open _____'s eyes and turn him/her from darkness to light, and from the power of Satan to You, God, that _____ might receive the forgiveness of sins and be sanctified. (Acts 26:18)

Father, I pray that _____ will make a genuine commitment to Jesus Christ as the Lord and Savior of his/her life. (Luke 14:25-27)

God, I pray that _____ would know You and receive the comfort of Your Presence while facing any dark valley. Help _____ to trust You and not be afraid. (Psalm 23:4)

Lord God, let _____ know that every word of Yours is flawless and that You are a shield to those who put their trust in You. (Proverbs 30:5)

Thank you, Father, that when _____ calls on You, You will be faithful and just and will forgive _____ and purify him/her from all unrighteousness. (I John 1:9)

Lord, I ask that You will set _____ free and that he/she will know freedom indeed. (John 8:36)

Open _____'s eyes, Lord Jesus, and show him/her the way of peace. (Isaiah 59:8)

Father, thank you for the day _____ will say "This is my God; I trusted in Him and He saved me. This is the Lord, I trusted in Him, let us rejoice and be glad in His salvation". (Isaiah 25:9)

Week One Notes

week two

Listen People To Christ

Some of our most basic needs are to understand and be understood. The best way to understand people is to listen to them.

Listening + Purposeful Questions = Meaningful Faith Conversations

The Listening Process

1. Listen and pray

2. Establish common ground

» Listen to find out where on the path they are now.

» Ask questions about family, occupation, where they were raised, hobbies, sports, etc.

3. Establish trust

» Use questions from their background and statements related to feelings, i.e. "How did it make you feel when your dad left your family?"

» Affirm "That must have been a frustrating time in your life" or "You must have felt pretty low after that", etc.

4. Understand their spiritual interests and beliefs

» Ask questions, i.e. "I guess I don't know much about your religious background" or "Were you raised in a religious home?", etc.

» You could share an element of your own religious background if it applies/relates to theirs in some way.

Gospel Presentation

- Make the Gospel clear. Be ready to answer common objections.

- Ask questions, such as, "Do you sense you are moving toward a personal relationship with God?" or "What would need to happen in your spiritual life for you to take the next step?", etc.

Five Steps in the Postmodern Path to Faith
(from I Once Was Lost by Don Everts and Doug Schaupp)

1. **Trusting a Christian** – moving from mistrust to trust

2. **Becoming Curious** – moving from complacent to curious

3. **Open to Change** – move from being closed to change to being open to change

4. **Seek After God** – move from meandering to seeking

5. **Entering the Kingdom** – repent, believe, and give their life to Jesus

Mark 4:26-29 shows the importance of understanding this path to faith as a "process" with different stages of growth, helping us love our non-Christian friends wisely and sensitively. Understanding this ushers you into a humble place of wonder and prayer.

Listening Is An Art

The better we listen, the better we serve people on their spiritual journey.

Listening Skills

1. Listen Attentively

- Make sure your body language and facial expressions assure them you are listening.
- Be responsive to what they are saying; show emotions such as empathy or joy.
- Good listening is a waiting skill.
- Do not necessarily give advice.
- Be truly interested in what they have to say.
- Build bridges for a deeper discussion.

2. Listen Adaptively

- Listen to the other person's concerns and questions. Walk alongside them, be present.
- Listening adaptively gives the other person space to see, reflect, consider and trust.
- Too often we become so focused on what is right in front of us (the next decision, the next goal) that we don't find the space or the time to listen adaptively.

Intentional Faith Conversations

The Ranch Fire in California was started from a hammer driving a metal stake into the ground. A common hammer, an ordinary stake, a few strikes... a transformed landscape. Think of it! You, God's story, a few courageous words... a transformed life. Take the risk.

Advantages of Asking Good Questions

- Sincere questions are friendly and flattering, showing genuine interest in the person and their ideas.

- Good questions can put you in the driver's seat of a conversation; they allow you to make progress on a point without being pushy.

- A question like "What do you mean by that?" can help you get deeper into a conversation. It clarifies the person's meaning so you don't misunderstand or misrepresent it.

- Everyone craves community; therefore, asking good questions can help you get to know one another. You can even go first and volunteer your answers to get things rolling.

Asking Good Questions

Sample questions that you can use in a conversation to transition into a faith dialogue. For example:

- What has your faith or spiritual journey been like?

- How are you dealing with what you are going through? How do you cope?

- How has this experience affected your view of God?

- Have you ever tried praying? What happened?

- What was your home life like growing up? Did you talk about God or go to church?

- What was your understanding of who Jesus is?

Responding to Difficult Questions

Q: What if my friend asks me a question such as "Why does a good God allow evil and suffering?"

A: We do not have an adequate answer for the problems of evil, no one does; we simply must have the honesty to admit it.

....

Q: What if my friend asks me a question that I don't know how to answer?

A: Take a moment to think, listening for how the Holy Spirit guides you to answer. Ask Him to take away your anxiety. It is okay to say, "I don't know, but let's explore that together."

....

Q: What if my friend asks me a controversial question that I feel uncomfortable answering?

A: It is okay to say "I prefer to talk about things that will unite us and not divide us. Do you mind if we talk about something else until we get to know each other better?"

....

Q: How do I avoid being perceived as a judgmental or hypocritical Christian by bringing up faith?

A: First, pray asking Jesus to take away your fears and to trust that when you step out in boldness, He will come through. Remember, it is always good to be vulnerable with your friend, admitting your own struggles in life and with faith. Sharing your story of what Jesus has done in your life is also a great way to relate to your friend.

Week Two Notes

week three

The Story of Now

**How are you experiencing Jesus
in the midst of your struggle?**
Friend · Comforter · Provider · Encourager

How are you relating to your friend?

REFLECT: Listen to Jesus

What is friendship with Jesus actually like?

How do you describe it?

How are you doing? (angry, sad, stressed, lonely, etc.)

What are you struggling with right now?

I am _____ because _____

_____

_____

_____.

Jesus has been _____ as I've struggled with _____

_____

_____

_____.

CONNECT: Listen to Your Friend

Questions to ask your friend to help you connect with them:

- How are you doing?

- How are you dealing with your struggles?

- What has helped?

INVITE: Listen to the Holy Spirit

Pray and ask the Holy Spirit to show you how to connect with your friend in a faith conversation.

Ask: "May I share how Jesus has made a difference in my struggles lately?"

Using discernment from the Holy Spirit, consider asking, "May I share how God's story can become real in your life?"

> "For I know the plans I have for you," says the Lord.
> "They are plans for good and not for disaster, to give you a future and a hope. In those days when you pray, I will listen. If you look for me wholeheartedly, you will find me."
> *Jeremiah 29:11-13*

Gospel Sharing Forces

This same Good News that came to you is going out all over the world. It is bearing fruit everywhere by changing lives, just as it changed your lives from the day you first heard and understood the truth about God's wonderful grace.

Colossians 1:6

The Process

1. Think of someone you are praying will become a believer in Christ. Write in their name and the date.

2. Ask "What are the positive forces that currently draw this person towards Jesus?" Write down the top three ideas in the "positive" column.

3. Now ask "What are the negative forces that currently draw this person away from Jesus?" Write down those three ideas in the "negative" column.

4. Brainstorm with your group actions that could double the impact of positive forces and lessen the impact of the negative forces.

5. On the bottom section write down three action steps you can intentionally take when you get together with your friend again to draw that person one degree closer to Jesus.

Worksheet example:

Name: *Pat*   **Date:**

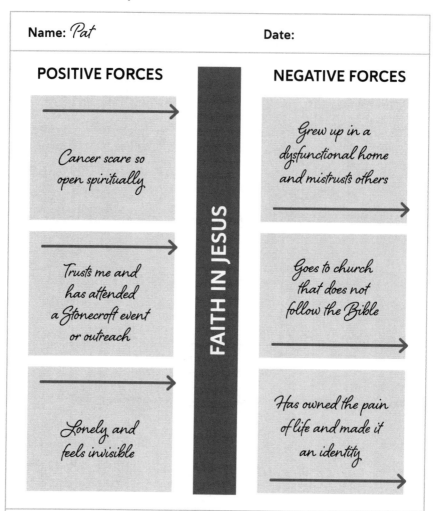

POSITIVE FORCES

Cancer scare so open spiritually

Trusts me and has attended a Stonecroft event or outreach

Lonely and feels invisible

FAITH IN JESUS

NEGATIVE FORCES

Grew up in a dysfunctional home and mistrusts others

Goes to church that does not follow the Bible

Has owned the pain of life and made it an identity

TOP THREE FOLLOW UP ACTIONS:

1. *Ask if they are open to join a prayer journey with me to heal broken places in our lives.*

2. *Invite him/her to explore questions about faith with me and ask if he/she would like to look at Jesus' teachings together.*

3. *Explore the Gospel if he/she is interested.*

Name: **Date:**

POSITIVE FORCES

FAITH IN JESUS

NEGATIVE FORCES

TOP THREE FOLLOW UP ACTIONS:

1.

2.

3.

Week Three Notes

week four

Sharing His Story

**Always be prepared to give an answer
for the hope that is within us. But do
this with gentleness and respect.**

1 Peter 3:15

Three essential elements to having a relationship with Jesus Christ:

ADMIT – Understand that sin **separates us from God**. Everyone is a sinner who needs forgiveness. (Romans 3:23)

BELIEVE – Realize that **Jesus is God's Son who came to our rescue.** Jesus wasn't just a good and wise person who used to live on this earth. He lived a sinless life, yet willingly died for our sins so we wouldn't have to. Three days later He came back to life. (Romans 10:9-10)

CONFESS – When we confess our sins, **God forgives us, removes our guilt and gives us peace.** We will have eternal life with Him in Heaven. (1 John 1:9)

**Imagine how this world would be
transformed if you and I and every other
person who knows God's story would
TAKE IT, LIVE IT, and TELL IT!**

FIX THIS MESS

Take a clean, crisp piece of paper representing how God created humanity in the beginning without sin.

- Explain that we all have sinned, and our paper is crumbed and ruined.

- Give the crumbled paper to the other person and say "Now, fix it! Make it perfect once again." Wait for their response (impossible).

- Explain how religion says, "Fix this mess you have." But Jesus says, "I'll take your paper and give you MY perfect paper instead."

DO VS. DONE

This is for someone raised in the church who doesn't understand the difference between religion and Christianity.

- Explain that religion is spelled D-O and Christianity is spelled D-O-N-E.

- Religion is about trying to do enough good things to please God.

- Christianity is based on the fact that Jesus has done it all. He lived a perfect life yet died on the cross to pay for our sins.

- His resurrection proved He is the one true God and makes eternal life with Him possible.

FOUR RELATIONSHIPS:
We were all created for relationship.

STEP 1 – Created for relationship: *Draw 5 circles. In the middle circle put yourself, then draw 4 circles around you and explain that each of us has relationship with*:

- **Myself/your internal self:** mental health, sense of purpose, anxiety, insecurity, self-image, etc.

- **Earth/your external self:** physical body, disease, finances, loss, physical needs of shelter, food, etc.

- **Others:** family, friends, marriage, co-workers, neighbors, etc.

- **God:** view of God, spiritual beliefs

Connect each outside circle to the middle circle with a line. Explain that in some of those relationships we are thriving and in some we are struggling.

STEPS 1 AND 2

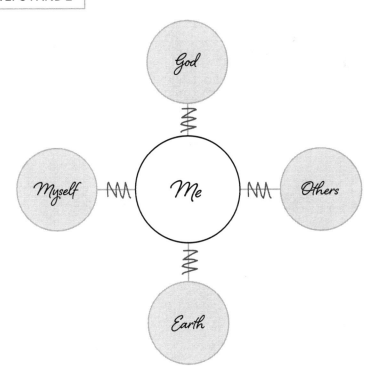

STEP 2 – Sin brought brokenness and barriers: *Draw squiggly lines over the line between each relationship:*

- Share that, because of sin – our sin, and the sins of others – each of those relationships has been damaged and cannot be fixed on its own.

- This sin leads to death and eternal separation from God.

STEP 3 – Jesus' death on the cross provides restoration: *Draw a heavy line between the circles (becomes shape of a cross).*

- God sent His Son, Jesus, who was perfect, to die a cruel death – providing an opportunity for restoration with others, our external and internal selves, and with God.

- He not only died, but He arose three days later proving He was God. All that Jesus went through on this earth He did for us because He wanted a personal relationship with us.

- A restored relationship with God is a gift. We don't work for it. All we need to do is trust that He is God, repent of our sin, and ask Jesus to be our restorer and the leader of our life.

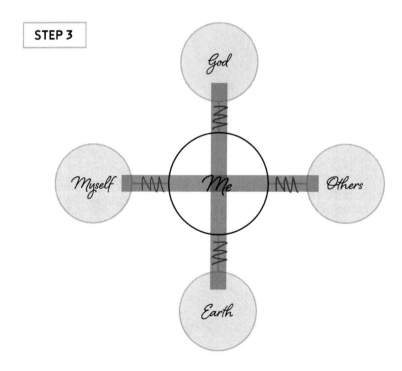

Week Four Notes

prayer journal

PRAYING FOR

DATE

HOW DO I KNOW THIS PERSON?

MY PRAYER FOR THEIR SALVATION

UPDATES & PRAYERS

/ / ....
....
....

/ / ....
....
....

/ / ....
....
....

/ / ....
....
....

_____ SAID "YES!" TO JESUS _____
NAME   DATE

PRAYING FOR

DATE

HOW DO I KNOW THIS PERSON?

MY PRAYER FOR THEIR SALVATION

UPDATES & PRAYERS

/ /

/ /

/ /

/ /

_____ SAID "YES!" TO JESUS _____

NAME   DATE

PRAYING FOR

DATE

HOW DO I KNOW THIS PERSON?

MY PRAYER FOR THEIR SALVATION

UPDATES & PRAYERS

/ / ....
....
....

/ / ....
....
....

/ / ....
....
....

/ / ....
....
....

_____ SAID "YES!" TO JESUS _____

NAME   DATE

PRAYING FOR

DATE

HOW DO I KNOW THIS PERSON?

MY PRAYER FOR THEIR SALVATION

UPDATES & PRAYERS

/ / ....
....
....

/ / ....
....
....

/ / ....
....
....

/ / ....
....
....

_____ SAID "YES!" TO JESUS _____
NAME   DATE

PRAYING FOR

DATE

HOW DO I KNOW THIS PERSON?

MY PRAYER FOR THEIR SALVATION

UPDATES & PRAYERS

/ /

/ /

/ /

/ /

_____ SAID "YES!" TO JESUS _____

NAME

DATE

PRAYING FOR

DATE

HOW DO I KNOW THIS PERSON?

MY PRAYER FOR THEIR SALVATION

UPDATES & PRAYERS

/ / ....
....
....

/ / ....
....
....

/ / ....
....
....

/ / ....
....
....

_____ SAID "YES!" TO JESUS _____
NAME   DATE

PRAYING FOR

DATE

HOW DO I KNOW THIS PERSON?

MY PRAYER FOR THEIR SALVATION

UPDATES & PRAYERS

/ /

/ /

/ /

/ /

_____ SAID "YES!" TO JESUS _____

NAME

DATE

PRAYING FOR

DATE

HOW DO I KNOW THIS PERSON?

MY PRAYER FOR THEIR SALVATION

UPDATES & PRAYERS

/ / ....
....
....

/ / ....
....
....

/ / ....
....
....

/ / ....
....
....

_____ SAID "YES!" TO JESUS _____
NAME   DATE

PRAYING FOR

DATE

HOW DO I KNOW THIS PERSON?

MY PRAYER FOR THEIR SALVATION

UPDATES & PRAYERS

/ /

/ /

/ /

/ /

_____ SAID "YES!" TO JESUS _____
NAME   DATE

PRAYING FOR

DATE

HOW DO I KNOW THIS PERSON?

MY PRAYER FOR THEIR SALVATION

UPDATES & PRAYERS

/ /

/ /

/ /

/ /

_____ SAID "YES!" TO JESUS _____

NAME

DATE

PRAYING FOR

DATE

HOW DO I KNOW THIS PERSON?

MY PRAYER FOR THEIR SALVATION

UPDATES & PRAYERS

/ /

/ /

/ /

/ /

_____ SAID "YES!" TO JESUS _____

NAME

DATE

PRAYING FOR

DATE

HOW DO I KNOW THIS PERSON?

MY PRAYER FOR THEIR SALVATION

UPDATES & PRAYERS

/ /

/ /

/ /

/ /

_____ SAID "YES!" TO JESUS _____
NAME   DATE

PRAYING FOR

DATE

HOW DO I KNOW THIS PERSON?

MY PRAYER FOR THEIR SALVATION

UPDATES & PRAYERS

/ /   ....
....
....

/ /   ....
....
....

/ /   ....
....
....

/ /   ....
....
....

_____ SAID "YES!" TO JESUS _____

NAME   DATE

PRAYING FOR

DATE

HOW DO I KNOW THIS PERSON?

MY PRAYER FOR THEIR SALVATION

UPDATES & PRAYERS

/ / ....
....
....

/ / ....
....
....

/ / ....
....
....

/ / ....
....
....

_____ SAID "YES!" TO JESUS _____

NAME

DATE

Made in the USA
Columbia, SC
15 April 2024

34196002R00030